Pitching Products

Products

For Small Business

eBook edition

As a buyer of the print edition of *Pitching Products For Small Business* you can now download the eBook edition free of charge to read on an eBook reader, your smart phone or your computer. Simply go to: **http://ebooks.brightwordpublishing.com/pitching** or using your smart phone, point it at the below.

You can then register and download your eBook copy of the book.

www.brightwordpublishing.com

Pitching Products

For Small Business

How to successfully prepare your
business, brand and products,
and sell to retail buyers

By Laura Rigney

A Brightword book
www.brightwordpublishing.com

HARRIMAN HOUSE LTD
3A Penns Road
Petersfield
Hampshire
GU32 2EW
GREAT BRITAIN

Tel: +44 (0)1730 233870
Fax: +44 (0)1730 233880
Email: enquiries@harriman-house.com
Website: www.harriman-house.com

First published in Great Britain in 2011 by Harriman House.

ISBN: 978-1-908003-17-1

British Library Cataloguing in Publication Data

A CIP catalogue record for this book can be obtained from the British Library.

Contents

About the author

Laura Rigney has been in sales all of her working life. After meeting various individuals who had developed fantastic products but who were unsure of the next step to take in selling these to stores, she realised there was a gap in the market for someone to help businesses do this. She set up Pitcher House with the sole aim of helping individuals get their products listed by major retailers.

Since the launch of her business, Laura has helped many individuals achieve a listing with some of the biggest high street names and international distributors.

Preface

What this book covers

The aim of this book is to help you get your business's products stocked by retailers, small and large. We will look at every type of retailer from small independent boutiques right through to nationally-known high street names. We will look at how to generate sales of your product from your own website, then sell to other online retailers, and then how to get your products stocked with distributors and physical, bricks and mortar stores.

Before approaching buyers there are many things that need to be considered – these can be the difference between success and failure. We will look at all of the preparation required before approaching and pitching to retailers so that you will have the best possible chance of success when you come to pitch your product.

Who this book is for

This book is for anyone who has developed a product that they believe has the potential to be successful and which they wish to see stocked in stores. Whether you're a start-up business that doesn't know where to begin when selling a product to stores, or an established company that is simply branching out into selling something new, there is something useful in this guide for every business at every stage of development.

How this book is structured

In Part One we look at planning and preparation before you pitch. We begin by ensuring you have everything you need in place, such as product protection, packaging and distribution. I also explain what market research you need to do both for your product and the buyers themselves.

Part Two deals with interactions with buyers, including the actual presentation of your products.

In Part Three we look at what you should do after you have pitched and successfully got your products stocked with retailers. The hard work does not stop there!

Introduction

For individuals who have invented or designed a product, or businesses that distribute other people's products, one of the most commonly asked questions is: "How do I approach and pitch to buyers?"

It's a very important question. I've heard it said that a buyer makes up their mind whether or not they will place an order within 30 seconds of the start of a sales pitch. This means that when pitching you have a very short window in which to grab a buyer's attention and make them take notice of you and your product.

So, what is the best way to do this?

I will answer this question by guiding you step by step through the route to market, from the product idea stage right through to your first buyer order. In doing so we will lay the foundations for successful future pitches and repeat orders.

Getting your products onto the hallowed shelves of high street stores and having your product featured on their websites – which receive as much business as the physical stores – requires a lot of planning and hard work even before you approach a retailer.

This can certainly seem daunting to begin with, but there are some simple tricks, techniques and shortcuts that can help you obtain orders from high street and online retailers. There are obstacles but, if handled correctly, these can be overcome.

If you follow the steps laid out in this guide, you will save time, money and energy, and you will create a good reputation amongst buyers.

Topics we will cover include:

- How to ensure you have a strong brand.
- The correct sales methods for your product.
- The research required, i.e. market research, industry research and retailer backgrounds, etc, and how to conduct this research.

- How to get the buyers to place that first order.
- What you should do after your products stocked with retailers to maintain and grow your business.

Case studies from buyers describing what they expect and what they dislike from those pitching to them, and from individuals who have successfully had their products stocked by leading retailers, are included. By reading these you can learn the secrets – of both success and failure – of those who have been through this process before, enabling you to learn from the experiences of others.

Part One

Before You Pitch

In Part One we will look at the preparation that needs to be done before you are ready to pitch your product. This involves:

- Preparing your product.
- Reviewing the methods for selling your product.
- Research into target retailers, buying departments and buyers.

Chapter 1

Preparing Your Product

Build a brand

Branding your product and your business correctly is vital when it comes to pitching. This is the first thing a buyer notices and a weak brand translates into a weak product.

There are a number of different definitions of what a *brand* actually is. It can refer to a business name, a product name, or a unique identifier such as a logo or trademark. The most effective description is that a brand is a name or symbol that is commonly known to identify a business or its products.

Your business's branding, therefore, is its message to the world. This will become the single thing that distinguishes you from others and will become the equivalent of your business's word. It is the promise of value that you make to the consumer, whether stated directly or simply implied.

A strong brand can command a premium price and maximise the number of units that can be sold at that premium. A weak brand can irreparably damage your image long term. For these reasons branding can make or break your product and this is definitely something that you need to invest both time and money in.

A well-known brand is generally regarded as one that people will recognise, regardless of whether they know about the products or services the business provides. Many people will recognise a logo and be able to match it up with a business or product without even thinking about it.

This kind of unconscious action signals a strong, well-marketed brand. This is not by any means an accident. When a business is planning their branding they have to go through many stages and may not always get it right first time.

For example, soft drink 7Up started life as a very different brand. Invented in 1929, it was originally named Bib-Label Lithiated Lemon Lime Sodas, which doesn't exactly roll off the tongue. The name was quickly changed to "7Up Lithiated Lemon-Lime", though this was still not quite catchy enough to grab people's attention.

Eventually, the name 7Up was settled upon – simple, easy to recall and, now, a household name. Throughout the renaming process, the product itself did not change, however without those early changes being made, 7Up might not have become the world famous, trusted brand that it has grown to become today.

How people perceive and feel about your product or business

Branding creates trust and an emotional attachment to your product or business. This attachment then causes customers to make decisions based, at least in part, upon emotion. Customers do not necessarily choose products for logical or intellectual reasons.

When thinking of the image you wish your brand to portray, try to imagine the emotions and perceptions that you want to evoke in your target market. Think about the emotions you want people to go through when they envisage your brand, then use this thought process in your brand planning.

Take a well-known brand like Jimmy Choo shoes. We associate Jimmy Choo with quality, high end, longevity, indulgence and luxury. The fact that people make these associations is no accident. Behind each well-known brand name there is a lot of planning, research and thought given to how the desired reaction can be created among consumers.

The first step to take with your own branding is to sit down and make a list of all the feelings you want the consumer to experience when they see your branding. You might choose words such as:

Quality, luxury, indulgence, high-end, deluxe, affluence, extravagance, impressive and opulence.

Or at the other end of the scale you might want your brand to be thought of as:

Low cost, good value and economical.

Once you have decided upon the reaction you want your brand to evoke you can then start to look at ways in which you can stir up these emotions in your target consumer. A graphic designer and brand expert will come in handy here. The main points for consideration are your business branding and your product branding.

A good designer can use fonts, colours, graphics and special effects to create the brand you are striving for. From your brief, they will create a number of different designs to fit your requirements, from which you can choose your favourite.

The best way to find a designer is to get recommendations from others. Take a look at the brands of other businesses that are in the same sort of area as you, or look out for a business whose branding you think achieves its aim, and then contact them to ask for the details of their designer. There's no reason why they shouldn't be more than happy to give you the details.

Some examples of graphic designers for small businesses that might be able to help you are Qwerty Cow (**www.qwertycow.com**) and Flourish Design (**www.flourishstudios.co.uk**).

You should consider that you may need some separate and slightly different branding for each of your products. For this reason, it is good to have a logo that can be easily tweaked so that you can expand your product range and accommodate new product ideas in the future.

Widening your product range

Keira O'Mara started her business, like most of us, with just one product, the Mamascarf – an aide for breast-feeding in public. When she started her journey Keira only required the name Mamascarf as she only had one product in her range, but since then she has gone on to develop a new product and has had to make a few changes. The business is now registered as Mamadesigns Limited and each individual product produced can have its own branding and identity whilst still maintaining the identity of the original Mamascarf brand.

www.mamascarf.co.uk

Key factors in a brand image

Simon Middleton, founder of the brand advisory firm Brand Strategy Guru, and author of *Build A Brand In 30 Days* and *What You Need To Know About Marketing*, says that there are several key factors that need to be taken into consideration when you are deciding upon your brand image:

- *Be authentic*. Authenticity means that a brand should not pretend to be something that it isn't. Brands should be true to themselves, otherwise they will be found out.
- *Be compelling*. A brand must be compelling to the senses, the emotions, the intellect or the imagination. Data alone is never compelling.
- *Be distinctive (unlike any competitor)*. Distinctiveness is what people are endlessly seeking. Nobody ever built a brand by being just like the other guys.
- *Build on excellence*. Businesses have to be very good at what they do. Apple, Google, Coke, etc., got to be great brands not by being average, but by being excellent.

- *Take an outsider's view.* Look at your brand from the outside and ask yourself: why would you buy or stock this business's products?

Think long and hard before making any firm decisions and use market research to help gather public opinion before committing to your branding. You do not want to be stuck with an image that you start to dislike very quickly or, worse still, that the consumer starts to dislike. Ensure your brand has the strength to go the distance.

Packaging

Part of your brand is the point of sale packaging of your product. Take some time to think about how your product will look when shown in a catalogue, when sitting on a shelf or when displayed on a website. Quite often people buy with their eyes so you really need to ensure that your product and its packaging is attractive in appearance.

You should make sure there is a clear message within your packaging. It needs to show an image of what's inside (if there is no option for a clear window), the product name, a description of use, any tag lines or phrases that you are using in marketing and your branding. Two companies that can help you with this are: Skylab Design (**www.skylabdesign.co.uk**) and Peachtree (**www.peachtree.uk.com**).

There are some legal aspects of packaging which must be adhered to and they vary from sector to sector. An experienced packaging agency will be able to advise you of the legal requirements. If you're unsure of your obligations then check with the Trading Standards Institute (**www.tradingstandards.gov.uk**) or at **www.legislation.gov.uk**.

If there are already products of a similar nature on the market, then it's well worth visiting the website or physical store of a stockist to take a look at how these products are displayed in their packaging. Make a note of the type of packaging used, the graphics and text used, and the quality of the finished packaging. How could you improve upon their design? When you look at their packaging can you see anything that you would add or remove? Think like a customer not an inventor.

One final thing to think about is the space stores have available. Most stores have shelving space but very little hanging space and some may have specifications for the size of products they can carry. Waterstones, for example, do not like awkward sized books. So, consider how your product's packaging will affect how stores can display it and explain to your packaging designer just how you see the product being displayed in store.

For many new products, the costs of packaging can be high and it's rare to find a company that will create a sample for you. They should, however, provide you with a three-dimensional PDF mock-up which you can use in your presentation. Providing the retailer can get a idea of the final size and appearance of the packing from the mock-up, it's perfectly acceptable practice to use a sample in this way.

Market research

It is vital when pitching your product that you can provide evidence of demand for it. In order to prove this you will need to carry out extensive market research *before* you pitch.

In addition to helping with your pitch, understanding your target market will help your business to sell its products. You can't make assumptions about what potential customers want so it's important to do some digging and learn about your customer's' interests and needs through market research. This information will also help you when it comes to future product development.

When conducting your research keep an open mind and do not be offended easily. There will almost certainly be people out there who hate your product idea and can see no point in the product being available, just as there will be people who love the product and wonder how they ever lived without it.

If you are worried about those you question stealing your idea then you could spend money on intellectual property protection or patents. Please see the later section on trademarks for more detail on this.

When people comment on your products or make suggestions for improvements, listen carefully and take their ideas on board. Keep a list of all suggestions and potential improvements that are mentioned – you may not necessarily agree with them at that point in time but you may find the comments useful when you refer back to them at a later date or look to develop a newer version or new product lines.

Some of the key things you need to learn about your target market include:

- *The demographics of your target customers*, including: age, gender, occupation, household income, disposable income, geographic location, and hobbies and interests. Add to this list anything else that could be relevant to potential sales for your type of product.

- *How big the market is.* This means annual revenues your competitors are currently generating, or your projection of potential customers and market size if you are introducing a completely new product. This information can be found in a company's annual reports. Remember to record your sources as you may need to provide evidence of how you arrived at these figures later.

- *The projected market size in five to ten years.* To deduce this you must look at the figures you have already obtained for the current market size and find figures from the previous years. Work out how much the market grew, or how much it shrunk, year on year for the last three to four years. Do allow for the impact of events such as ash clouds, financial catastrophes, bad weather, etc., in your calculations. Table 1.1 provides an example of the sort of data you might collect.

Table 1.1 – example of revenue growth in a business over four years

Trading Year	Revenue	Growth %
1	200,000	n/a
2	350,000	75%
3	644,000	84%
4	1,197,840	86%

- Once you have the previous years figures you need to *work out the average revenue growth*. Using the figures for the example business in Table 1.1 that would be 82% ((75% + 84% + 86%)/3 = 82%). When you have this figure you can use it to estimate the market growth potential year on year for the next three years. Use this figure for market growth potential to make projections for future sales. Once more, an explanation of your journey from your initial figures to your projections is essential, so keep a record of your calculations.

- *Specific groups within your target market* on which you want to focus some special marketing attention, for example babies and children, young professionals, specific age groups, specific professions, etc. You need to know why this sector is of particular interest to you, and how this will benefit the brand and increase sales of your product.

How to do your own market research

Market research can be a costly exercise if carried out by a professional company but there are many ways in which you can do your own constructive research without having to spend too much money.

An online survey

A really easy way to start your research is by using online survey sites such as SurveyMonkey (**www.surveymonkey.com**) or Constant Contact (**www.constantcontact.com/online-surveys**). Both are free to use and allow you up to 100 results per survey.

With 100 respondents you will have enough data to get a general view, providing the people answering your questions are from within your target demographic (you can check this by including optional and anonymous questions on sex, age and income). They also allow you to look at the results as an overall report as well as showing individual responses. This should give you an in-depth understanding of your survey respondents.

How to structure your survey questions

When creating your survey you should:

- *Keep questions clear and precise.* Nothing is more off-putting for someone taking the survey than having to re-read a question a number of times to try to achieve an understanding of just what it's actually asking.
- *Keep questions short.* A sure way to deter people from completing your survey is to ask them to write a 3000 word essay on the positive and negative aspects of your product.
- *Beware of bias!* By this I mean ensure that the wording of your question does not point to a preference for a certain answer. Survey respondents may subconsciously want to please you and so may follow the lead if one is given within the question. If this occurs it will render your results useless.
- *Ensure the survey can be feasibly completed in five minutes.* If it takes longer than five minutes, you run the risk of participants losing patience and giving any answer to simply finish the survey.

Where to find people to take your survey

Social networking sites are good sources of people to participate in surveys. Sites like Twitter (**www.twitter.com**), Facebook (**www.facebook.com**) and LinkedIn (**www.linkedin.co.uk**) all have groups or lists of people that are interested in certain subjects, activities or interests. Simply post in group discussion areas with a link to your survey asking people to complete it. As an added incentive you can offer a prize for participants. This can be something small and easy to post or email like a gift voucher to be won after a prize draw of all survey participants.

You can also try to find relevant online forums and organisations that allow you to post links to your survey. Forums are very popular and a great way to get in front of your target market. If you have a baby product, for example, sign up to some parenting forums and ask other users for their feedback.

And there you have it, for as little as one hour's work and an outlay of £10 for a high street gift voucher, you will have started your own market research.

Focus groups

Focus groups are another way to evaluate products or concepts to learn how well they'll be received by your target audience. Ask your family, friends, and friends of friends, to the group session, aiming to assemble a diverse range of people that fits within your target market. Remember that a focus group can be as small as five or ten people; the figure is irrelevant providing it consists of your target consumer demographic. If using family or friends make it quite clear from the outset that you will not be offended by any opinions, suggestions or responses provided (and then remember not to be offended!).

Focus groups can take place somewhere informal such as your own home. Invite your group over for coffee or lunch – you'll find the results you receive will far outweigh the cost of playing host. Have a list of questions ready to ask that will provide you with the evidence you need. Once you have your audience's attention, present your product to them, and ask for their opinions on things such as:

Is the price point realistic? Would they pay that amount or would they consider it an extravagance?

What would they change about the product and why? How do they feel the changes would enhance the existing product?

What would make the product more appealing, either to them individually or to an alternative and possibly wider audience?

Market research is something that must be done. When you are pitching to buyers they will ask you many questions about your market. The buyers themselves may or may not already know the answers to these questions – this may be their way of testing you, checking that you are serious and that you have done everything in your power to ensure you are ready for your pitch. It is important that you know the answers in order to impress buyers during your pitch, but also for your own product planning and development.

Funding

Starting a business and developing a product needs careful financial planning. As a first step, you need to establish whether you have enough capital already at your disposal or whether you will need funding. You also need to ensure that once you've pitched your product and received an order you will have the capital to fund production. You should start by making a list of all your costs.

Initial manufacturing costs

There is a misconception that before you approach retailers you need to have a warehouse full of stock ready to dispatch just in case you receive an order. Small businesses cannot start in this way because few of them have spare money in the initial stages to produce a lot of stock in the hope that they receive an early order.

With some products a sample will work just as well as the finished article when you are pitching, provided your sample is of good quality and looks like the finished product. If the product is an invention of your own then you may not need much money to get started. You probably already have a prototype or some technical drawings that can be worked from so your first step is to identify a manufacturer and then contact them with a view to getting a sample. This is also a way of vetting manufacturers, which we will come back to later.

Most manufacturers should be more than happy to create a sample product for you. After all, they are aware that businesses will not place an order for 20,000 units of an item without being absolutely certain that the manufacturer can produce a single item to the quality that they require.

If you build up a good rapport with a manufacturer, you may be able to convince them that it would be mutually beneficial to agree to a small manufacturing run initially. If you can get 20 or so units of a high quality at a reasonable price, these can be used as samples and sent out to potential buyers.

Funding for your business

If you think you are going to require funding you need to think about what types of funding are available to you and which would work best for you in the long term. Table 1.2 shows the pros and cons of different types of funding.

Table 1.2 - weighing up types of funding

Type of funding	Pros	Cons
Bank loan	Large amounts available. Fixed interest rate. Repayable over long period.	Very difficult to acquire. Interest rates can be high.
Private investment	Large amounts available. Potential guidance from experienced investor. More flexible agreements available.	Can mean giving away a share of your business in return for funding. Can be difficult to find a suitable investor.
Grant	If repayable, usually only a low interest rate and low repayments required.	Very difficult to find an applicable grant.

Bank loans might be considered the most obvious method of funding, but they can be difficult to acquire and can saddle your business with long-term debt. However, there are alternatives if you are prepared to look for these opportunities.

Many people overlook private investment as an option for start-ups but it can be a realistic route to take. Bill Morrow, founder of Angels Den (**www.angelsden.co.uk**), says:

"The benefits of angel funding over bank funding are too many to mention. In 2011, angel funding is available, unlike bank funding. Angels Den operates across the UK and receives over 100 business plans a day and talks to 250 entrepreneurs a month in each of its nine regions.

"We have not heard of a new bank loan being extended in the past 15 months, while on the other hand angels are keen to give you

money in exchange for a percentage of your business. They want you to succeed as they are directly incentivised."

The other big difference between a loan and funding from private investors is that investors (or angels) are giving you the money – the business is not expected to pay it back. Instead, the investor swaps the money for a percentage of your business. If your business does badly they may not recoup their investment, but this is the risk they take. An additional benefit is that as the investor has put their own money into the business they may give you advice or provide you with access to useful contacts they have gained up in their years of business experience.

Another alternative to bank loans is a skill swap, providing it is carried out correctly. Try to connect with someone who has the skill set that you need for the next stage of your product development and see if they will work for you for free in return for you doing something for them in return. This may mean spending a day doing filing in their office or helping them out with some sales or marketing. If you both get something useful for nothing then you'll both be happy.

Once again, social networking sites such as Facebook, Twitter and LinkedIn can be used to find people to connect with in this way.

Supply and distribution

The manufacturing of your product will affect more than just the retail price. You have to consider details such as shipping times, communication problems and so on. Having products manufactured overseas can be much more cost effective but you must consider the difficulties that you may also encounter in the process, for example:

- *Communication.* Not only is there a language barrier but also a time difference. Are you happy to sit up until the early hours so that you can speak to your manufacturer?

- *Distance.* Before instructing a manufacturing run you should ideally be able to take a look around the factory and discuss their processing methods. This may not be possible if your manufacturer is overseas, so think about the sacrifices this may mean. If you do decide to visit a manufacturer that is some distance from where your business is based think about mounting expenses as you travel back and forth developing your working relationship.

- *Shipping.* If you are placing a large order with an overseas manufacturer you need to factor in the length of time it will take to reach the UK as well as the import charges and duties. Once these are added does it still make overseas manufacture feasible?

- *Quality.* If the finished products arrive and they not to the standard you require it will be time consuming and costly to resolve this issue if you have to register a complaint and then return the products to a foreign manufacturer.

If your product is a success and larger orders start to come in then it may be in your interest to look at manufacturing overseas as production costs tend to be lower, but in the initial stages it will more than likely be cost and time effective to try to find a UK-based manufacturer.

Once you have narrowed down your list of manufacturers you should visit each one to assess the working relationship that you can build with them. This is important to the success of your business and the end quality of your product.

Also, it's a good idea to have two principal manufacturers rather than one, just in case something should happen to prevent one of them delivering your goods. Imagine waking up one morning to find out there had been a fire at your manufacturer's factory, or that they had gone into liquidation! You need to have a contingency plan in place for such circumstances.

Insurance can cover your costs should the worst happen, but it may take a while to get payments from insurers so having a back-up supplier is the best kind of insurance.

Cash flow

When you are running a business, particularly in the early stages, you should be prepared to have a low level of working capital. You will need to plan carefully and should have some kind of back-up budget in place. Let's look at how this is relevant to pitching your products and receiving product orders.

Imagine the following scenario: You have a working budget of £5000 and following a successful pitch you receive an order with a value of £10,000. The cost of the merchandise to you is £5000 so you place your stock order with your manufacturer and pay in full knowing that you will soon receive payment of £10,000.

In between receiving your stock and sending it to your customer, you receive another order worth £3000, but as you have used all of your working capital on the initial order you are unable to pay the manufacturer and therefore cannot place the second order. This could lead to an unhappy customer and potentially a lost sale.

Don't forget that if you have agreed, for example, a four-week delivery time and 60-day payment terms, there could be three months between the order being placed and you receiving your payment. This is of course also dependant on you receiving payment on time.

If your cash flow is tight in the early stages of your business try to make your circumstances clear to your manufacturer – you may be able to find a solution. If you explain the position you are in and sign a contractual agreement you may be able to negotiate terms that are more suitable for you, or even just something temporary until your cash flow is more stable.

One method you might choose is to have different payment terms for your customers and your suppliers. For example, if you work on the basis that your delivery time is four weeks and you have 60 day payment terms with your manufacturer then putting in place 30 day payment terms with your customer means, if everything goes to plan, you should receive payment for the goods at around the same time as you are due to pay the manufacturer's invoice.

You should also ensure that you have a contingency budget available. I would never recommend using a credit card to order and pay for stock but if the facility is available and you are sure you will be able to clear the balance before it becomes liable for interest then it can become a useful interim solution.

Pricing

If you have used market research, consumer and competition, to determine the RRP of your product then this will help you justify your pricing to buyers.

Regardless of whether you are selling direct to the consumer or through a retailer your RRP should always remain consistent. Selling through your own website will generate a higher profit and may tempt you to lower the price to increase sales but by doing this you are potentially drawing consumers away from the retailers that you worked so hard to get orders from. In the long run, this may make the retailer wary of placing any additional orders if they feel sales have not been at a high enough volume.

There are no clear-cut rules when it comes to setting a price for your product but there are some methods you can use for guidance. You need to have three prices in mind at all times: your production cost, your wholesale price and your retail price.

There are three main calculations that can be used for setting your retail price:

- *Markup pricing.* When you created your business plan, if you decided that you wanted to make a 30% markup on each unit, for example, then the following calculation is the one to use. You add your markup to your cost price to get the wholesale price and then double the wholesale price to obtain the RRP. In this instance you are selling to the trade buyers at a 50% discount.

Cost price + 30% = wholesale price

Wholesale price x 2 = RRP

So, if your cost price is £1:

Wholesale price = £1 + 30% = £1.30

RRP = £1.30 x 2 = £2.60

- *Keystone pricing.* This is the traditional method of working out your RRP but it is not used as much as it used to be. It's by far the easiest method though and has the best margins. You simply double your cost price to obtain a wholesale price and then double this figure again to get the RRP. Therefore:

Cost price x 2 = wholesale price

Wholesale price x 2 = RRP

So, if your cost price is £1:

Wholesale price = £1 x 2 = £2

RRP = £2 x 2 = £4

- *Competitive pricing.* This can be the trickiest of the lot. This means following your competitors constantly and always ensuring you are undercutting them. The downside means a smaller profit but it also usually means higher sales. The calculations are slightly different as you work backwards from a competitor's price:

Competitor's price − 10% = RRP

RRP − 50% = wholesale price

Difference between wholesale price and cost = markup

So, if your competitor's price is £20 and your cost price is £5:

RRP = £20 - 10% = £18

Wholesale price = £18 - 50% = £9

Markup = £9 - £5 = £4

When deciding on the best pricing strategy to use you should always remember that as your business grows, so will your overheads, which will eat into any profit that you make. You don't want to set prices and then have to repeatedly increase them to cover the costs of running your business.

Neither, should you set your prices so high that you become uncompetitive with similar products. If pitching your products to a retailer they will be deterred from doing business with you if they think customers will deem your products to be overpriced.

Speak to a professional and ask them to look at your costing plan. There are a few government organisations such as Business Link (**www.businesslink.gov.uk**) who provide this service free of charge, or alternatively they will refer you to somebody else that can help.

Proof of sales potential

If you are in a position to start selling your products before approaching buyers, the results can be beneficial to your pitch. Racking up some sales on your own and stating to buyers that you have sold 'x' number of units will prove to buyers that given the right exposure and marketing, your product could potentially sell well. It will also demonstrate that your price point is realistic.

This will help to boost a buyer's confidence when they are considering placing an order with you. Use your past sales data to prove you are targeting the correct demographic.

Product protection

Trademarks

Registering a trademark against your product or brand will prevent others from illegally copying it. This will be an incentive to buyers because it will give assurance that another business cannot reproduce your idea.

Typically, you can apply for a trademark on a name, word, phrase, logo, symbol, design, image or a combination of any of these elements. All the details you need are on the Intellectual Property Office website (**www.ipo.gov.uk/types/tm.htm**).

Obtaining a registered trademark for your brand or product is an expensive business, but you don't necessarily have to register the trademark for it to be effective.

There are two trademark symbols that you may recognise:

- ™ Shows that you intend to or already have started the application process to obtain a trademark.
- ® Shows that you have registered a trademark against your brand or name.

If you are the owner of a registered trademark you are protected against others using your trademarked brand or name by Trademark Infringement Law. However, this registration is not required. Once you have applied a ™ mark to your image, name or logo, you are covered under trademark common law. This may not provide as much protection as a registered mark but should be sufficient.

Before deciding on which route is best for you, I would advise speaking to a specialist trademark attorney (try **www.itma.org.uk**). You can usually get a little free advice over the phone if you go through an organisation such as Business Link.

Patents

A patent protects a new invention by covering many different aspects of the product, such as:

- How things work.
- What they do.
- How they do it.
- What they are made of.
- How they are made.

A patent essentially prevents others from taking your idea and producing it under their branding.

Patents can be expensive to obtain so you need to weigh up your options. If your product is unique or has some unique aspects to it, it may be better for you to simply patent those features rather than the entire product.

If you do have a genuinely original idea of process, the benefits of owning a patent could far outweigh the cost attached. Having protection on the technology or a different aspect of your invention means that you will be the only person with the authority to produce it and it instantly gives you a market edge.

As with trademarks it is advisable to obtain help from a professional patent attorney. All details are available from the Chartered Institute of Patent Attorneys (**www.cipa.org.uk**).

Further information about patents is available from the Intellectual Property Office (**www.ipo.gov.uk/types/patent.htm**).

Retailer case study

- **Name** – Keira O'Mara
- **Company** – Mama Designs Ltd (Mamascarf)
- **Position** – Director
- **Email** – info@mamascarf.co.uk

What, in your opinion, is the best way to get the name of the correct buyer for your product?

When I first made contact with companies, I would Google them to get their head office number and ask for the relevant buyer. Often they won't give a name over the phone but will advise you to send a letter introducing yourself and your product and asking them whether they would like to see a sample. Most companies will then reply, either by post or email.

Have you found any particular method that gets the attention of buyers via phone or email?

I think that it makes sense to follow the company guidelines, so if they ask you to send a letter it is best to do so, as they are inundated with queries and you don't want to annoy them. You do have to be persistent though – I have managed to successfully get into one major retailer by going back to them six months after my initial contact with an update (by email). I think that it is fine to follow up by email if you are waiting for a response and haven't heard anything for a while. I ask whether they have any feedback for me.

Were you asked any questions that you hadn't expected?

I have been asked by a buyer how many of my products I have sold within another retailer and which retailers are stocking Mamascarf.

Did you do anything to make your pitch stand out?

I have put together a folder detailing my media coverage and awards, so that buyers can see the support they can expect, as it is this that will make the product sell.

Was there a particular part of the pitching process that you found difficult? What solution did you find?

I have been lucky in that price negotiations have always been done by email. I think that I would have found this challenging to do face to face. Doing it by email allows you space to think and ensure that you don't make any wrong decisions. If I was asked to reduce my wholesale price in a face-to-face meeting, I would say that I would get back to them and follow up by phone or email within a few days.

If you could give one piece of advice about pitching a product to a retailer what would it be?

My advice would be to do your homework. Prepare in advance answers to every possible question that you think you might be asked or challenge you might be presented with. Also make sure you know about the retailer, their stores, their customers and the competitor's products they already stock. Talking negatively about your competitor's products is not a good idea – you need to be able to say why your product would complement their existing range.

Chapter 2

Methods for Selling Your Products

There are a number of ways to sell your products and you need to ensure that you are using each to its best potential, not only to increase sales but also to continue raising your brand awareness. Both will help when you come to pitch your products.

In this chapter we will look at four ways you can sell your products:

1. From your own website.
2. Through online retailers.
3. In independent stores.
4. Using a distributor.

As we move through these four stages we will look at how to put into practice important processes from the start, so that you are fully prepared to pitch to large retailers when the time comes.

1. Direct sales from your website

Selling your product directly to consumers is the best way to start making sales. The easiest and cheapest way to do this is online through your own website. You can plaster your own branding all over the site, have a page dedicated to other stockists with links to their websites, and you can include your contact details, including a phone number, to instil confidence in people who are looking to buy online.

Solvej Biddle, inventor of the Sleep Canopy and the TrayKit, uses her own website to attract new customers as well as selling into retail. She says:

"Direct contact with your consumers is essential to enable you to adapt your products to customer needs and to understand their product usage. If you only sell via retailers it is harder to gain this feedback. Ensure that you keep a good customer database and seek the comments and thoughts of your purchasing public. Selling direct also gives you a larger margin, which helps to redress the balance of large margins taken by the retailers. There are costs involved with maintaining your own e-commerce capability but the benefits outweigh the costs, certainly in the early days."

How to set up your website

If you intend to set up your own website and sell your products through it, your first step is to register a domain name. This is your website address. If you can get the same domain name as your business name then that's a great start. If your business name is unavailable then try using a hyphen. You can register a domain name for as little as £2.99 per year from companies such as 123-reg (**www.123-reg.co.uk**).

Once you have a domain name you will need to find a hosting company to provide you with the web space for your site. Companies that can provide this service include Heart Internet (**www.heartinternet.co.uk**) and Fast Hosts (**www.fasthosts.co.uk**).

Now that you have a domain name and some web space, you need to actually build your site. Websites can be very expensive if built by professionals but there are lots of affordable options you can use. For example, there are plenty of *out-of-the-box* websites available now which charge you an annual or monthly fee that includes your hosting too. These can cost you as little as £2.99 per month. Two examples of such services are Create (**www.create.net**) and Mr Site (**www.mrsite.co.uk**).

These websites begin as a template which you can customise to your taste and branding. You can have a number of pages and can even include an online shop to enable consumers to buy directly from you. Providers of online shopping carts that you can attach to your own site include GroovyCart (**www.groovycart.co.uk**), RomanCart (**www.romancart.com**) and CubeCart (**www.cubecart.com**). These allow customers to quickly and securely click and buy your products directly from your website.

If you choose to use a template website, it is worth putting a little money aside to have a professional do the design. You can make an out of the box website look great with just a little professional help. It shouldn't cost more than a couple of hundred pounds but will make a difference to the impact and impression that your site has to the consumer. How many times have you visited a website but left straightaway because it looks awful or it's simply too difficult to navigate? It is hard enough to get people to visit your site because of the number of sites competing for 'attention. Once you've achieved the goal of getting them to your website you don't want people to lose interest instantly just because your site does not look appealing.

Another benefit of having your own website is that you can get people to sign up to a mailing list and keep a database of your customers. You can then keep in touch with your customers regularly, informing them of any special offers you are running, any new retailers that are now stocking your products, or making them aware of any new products that you are launching.

In the long term you may wish to upgrade to a professionally designed website as you can then add extra features that don't always come with template websites. In the meantime, a template site is a cost-effective and easy way to start.

Other books you may find useful

In this book on pitching it is not relevant to go into more detail about how to set up and run your business website. However, for more information about setting up online and generating sales of your products through your site, you may find the following books useful:

- *The Start-Up Kit: Everything you need to start a small business*
- *Go Global: How to Take Your Business to the World*

Both books are by Emma Jones and are published by Brightword Publishing.

2. Online retailers

Online retailers can be hugely beneficial to your profits and to awareness of your brand. If your product is featured on their website it can increase your web presence dramatically.

To identify the most appropriate online retailers for your product, just have a little search. Type the sort of phrases that you would expect people to use when looking for your product into a search engine. The results of this search should give you a good starting point.

Visit each site and see whether you feel your product would sit comfortably within the current range offered there. Once you're happy, simply call the retailer and introduce yourself or send them an email explaining what you are proposing and asking what their normal buying arrangements are.

The more exposure your product and your brand have online the better it will perform in search engine results. This means that by getting your product into online stores you can save money on search engine optimisation (SEO) as your stockists will be doing it on your behalf.

SEO basics from Alison Rothwell

When you first start selling online, SEO (search engine optimisation) is a phrase you hear very often. Optimising your website brings you targeted traffic. This is traffic that you don't have to pay money to get (unlike using pay-per-click advertising).

Millions of people search online every single day for millions of things and most online purchases begin with the customer using search engines of some kind. In fact, over 90% of internet visitors use a search engine.

SEO also means the visitors to your site are more targeted, which in turn means more sales and higher conversion rates for you. It also helps you to develop a strong brand that is recognisable in your marketplace or your industry. Sites which rank highly in search engines give potential customers the impression that the website is a professional market leader. All of this will help when you come to pitch to buyers.

SEO comprises two main elements:

1. What you say about yourself – on-page elements – including meta description, keywords, navigational structure, etc.
2. What others say about you – backlinks – including those from directories, articles, social media platforms and networking sites.

Firstly, when preparing your website, think about your meta tags. This means that each and every page on your site should have its own unique title, description and keywords (25 or less per page). Remember to keep descriptions short, relevant and to the point.

You can see the meta tags for websites by clicking 'View' and then 'Page source' when browsing the internet. You might like to check what your competitors are up to, especially if their website performs well in search engine rankings.

You also need to build links to your website. One-way links are links from another website to yours, reciprocal links are where a site links to you and you link back. Links to your site can come from many sources – you can place links from online business directories, forums, articles or social networking sites, to name but a few.

The most important off-page factor to gain high Google rankings is appropriate anchor text pointing to the specific page of your website that has been optimised for a particular keyword phrase. Anchor text is that portion of a hyperlink that is viewed by a user on a webpage (the clickable text).

Alison Rothwell is an internet marketing expert and currently manages an online marketing consultancy. She can be reached at www.alisonrothwell.com where you can register for a free audio CD and sign up for her free e-zine for weekly search engine optimisation advice.

Drop shipping

You may want to consider offering a drop shipping service for your smaller retailers. Drop shipping basically means selling your goods through an online retailer without them ever holding physical stock. So, for example, drop shipping service **www.websiteA.com** will display and sell your products for you.

Whenever they make a sale they take the payment direct from the end customer and send you details of the orders received (usually once daily) and the customers who have made them. Once you have the order details you process the order and send the items directly to the customer yourself. You then invoice the retailer, using the drop shipping rate initially agreed (usually on a monthly basis) for the items sent.

Some businesses that sell their products through drop shipping are:

- Ella Announcements: **www.ellaannouncements.co.uk**
- Magic Whiteboard: **www.magicwhiteboard.co.uk**
- Rokka Play: **www.rokkaplay.com**
- Belle Belly: **www.bellebelly.co.uk**

The price charged to drop shippers can vary. It never goes as low as the wholesale price as they are not buying in bulk and you can never guarantee the level of orders that you will receive. I've known drop shipper discounts to be anything from 10% right up to 30% – it's completely at your discretion. But remember that whilst a high discount will encourage more drop shipper interest, you will be doing 95% of the work yourself so you should not pay the same fees as you would pay a distributor.

Donna Pinnell, owner of The Little Lilypad Co (**www.littlelilypad.co.uk**) sells many items from suppliers on a drop ship basis and says:

"Starting and running a business is no mean feat and keeping stock of every item on the website can be a costly option. The Little Lilypad Co chose to offer a range of personalised products and without employing additional staff to craft and create these items we looked to find suppliers who would design and produce these items and drop ship on our behalf. We have found this to be extremely successful and we have expanded the number of drop ship partners to enable us to offer our customers a wider range of products."

Using a drop shipper is a great way to get used to selling your products to businesses rather than consumers. Smaller online retailers are usually very open to new product suggestions as not only does it have the potential to increase revenue but it also broadens their existing product range. If you have a drop shipping option it means they can make a decision based on the fact that it's zero risk for them but potentially a source of very good returns for both of you.

3. Independent high street stores

Another way to generate interest and gauge the public reaction to your product is to approach small, independent stores. This will also give you practice at pitching your product to retailers.

Start locally and identify any small retailers in your area that you feel would benefit from stocking your product. Once you have a list of stores, get the name of the person you need to speak to. The easiest way to do this is to call and ask for the name of the business owner and when they will next be on the premises.

I have always found that the cheeky approach works well here. Small retailers are careful before spending money on new stock so trying to make an appointment for to sell your products to them can prove very difficult. If you have an idea of the days they are in the store, get your suit on, a sample in your hand and pay them a visit.

Just drop into the shop and introduce yourself to the person in charge. Explain that you realise this is probably a really busy time for them and that you're sure they have important things to do, but you would really appreciate them giving you five minutes to just take a look at your wonderful new product. Flattery and indulging their sense of self-importance really does work a treat so use it to your advantage.

This is an excellent way to work on your face-to-face selling skills. Don't forget, if you can see no reason why the retailer shouldn't stock your product and yet they still refuse, ask them why. They may offer an objection that you can answer, turn around, and possibly even turn into a sale.

The response may be something as simple as "We have no money for new stock." In this case you could also offer them the chance to trial your products on a sale or return basis. Leave them a small stock quantity of around ten units on the understanding that they display them for a two-week period. Once that time is up you can return to the retailer to see if they had demand.

If they have sold none of your products but state that they have had interest you may consider allowing them an extension of a fortnight. If they have sold nothing and return all of your stock then neither you nor the retailer have made a loss. If, however, they have sold some of your items and feel that the demand will grow you can invoice them for the full quantity and start to discuss terms to supply to them in the future on a normal wholesale basis.

This is a good way to test the local market. Once you have built up a portfolio of local stores that are regularly selling your products you should then begin looking slightly further afield using the same skills that you have already proven successful.

4. Distributors

The primary job of a distributor is to buy a product from the producer and resell it to the retailer. Their role is to find you more customers but, in essence, the distributor is your customer – possibly your most important customer.

You might need to use a distributor because some large retailers simply will not deal directly with a small producer. In fact, the store may even be willing to sacrifice some of their usual margin in order to avoid dealing with the producer.

It would be completely viable to run your business using distributor custom alone. Essentially, a distributor gets your product from the point of manufacture to the point of sale without you having to worry about too much in between.

Find the right distributor for you

Almost any type of retailer can build and grow a successful business if they manage to connect with the right wholesale distributor, but trying to establish which distributor is the right one for you can be difficult, especially if it is the first time you have entered the wholesale and distribution markets.

The key is research. Some sectors are overflowing with distributors so trying to identify the best one for you can be tough. Where you find there is a lot of choice, there's a good chance that the distributors can afford to be picky and will only deal with large companies, but this may even work in your favour.

When looking at distributors I would advise trying to find a small yet established organisation to work with. These types of distributors have spent time and effort building up relationships with buyers and are still small enough that they are personally cultivating those relationships. Remember, a small distributor does not necessarily have reduced buying power.

A great way to find details of relevant distributors is to ask others in a related field. You may have some contacts and useful friendships with other small businesses and these can be used as a source of information (though be aware that direct competitors may not wish to give you too much help here). Other businesses may have already established a distributor or even have come across one that they think may work well for your product, so never be afraid to ask. You may even find that someone is happy to make an initial introduction for you.

In some instances you may be able to find out who handles a company's distribution on that company's website. It is certainly worth checking.

Ideally you will find a distributor who already specialises within your industry. This way they already have the contacts needed to get your product listed with retailers and they will have a wealth of experience that they will probably be happy to share with you. However, try to avoid using a distributor that is already representing one of your competitors as this could lead to a conflict of interests.

There are many distributor directories available to purchase on the internet. Whilst some are a genuinely useful purchase, there are many that will be of very little use. Try to get recommendations before parting with any cash. Try searching on Google for the name of the business offering the directory to see if their service has been reviewed by other customers on business website forums.

Pros and cons of using distributors

Let's take a look at the pros and cons of using distributors:

Pros

- *Wide reach.* A distributor could make your product international without you having to deal with any of the logistical issues that come with global trading. A distributor usually deals with the shipment of the goods along with any export or customs problems.

- *Existing relationship network.* Distributors already have relationships with retailers. They are considered to be a reliable source of quality products and therefore get them listed faster and in larger quantities.

- *Marketing.* The marketing is now shared with the distributor. Don't forget, they also rely on selling your products so it's in their best interest to push them as much as possible.

- *Storage.* Distributors have their own storage and warehousing facilities, which reduces your costs.

- *Frees up your time.* Using a distributor leaves you more time to concentrate on the daily running of the business and future product development.

- *Reduced running costs.* Imagine selling 1000 single units and having to invoice, process and despatch each order individually. When you receive an order from a distributor for 1000 units it takes one invoice, one payment process and one delivery.

Cons

- *Reduced margin.* You lose a percentage of your profit as the distributor needs a margin when selling to retailers.

- *Retail price is out of your control.* You may find that the retail price is increased as this is no longer in your control. This could mean your product is priced out of the market.

- *Distance from customers.* By employing a distributor you are adding a link in the chain between you and your customers. You have to trust that the distributor will represent you and your products as well as you would yourself.

I believe the positives far outweigh the negatives when it comes to this kind of selling.

Pricing when using a distributor

When planning your pricing strategy you should factor in distributor involvement. As a rule of thumb, distributors work to a 10% - 15% profit margin. This may seem a lot when it's coming out of your pocket, but it soon repays itself as more sales channels are opened up for you.

Some distributors may charge more than this 10% and some may charge less, but don't be tempted to go with a distributor simply because they are slightly cheaper. Distributors really do work for their money and you should never underestimate the difference a great distributor can make to your business long term. I would be very wary of a distributor that promises the earth in return for a small fee.

Once you have identified your ideal distributor, you need to pitch your product to them. This is done in such a way that they can see the benefit to them, the retailer and the consumer. They have spent time and energy building up trusted relationships with buyers and will in no way want it tarnished by a product that does not live up to its promises.

You need to not only pitch the distributor the benefits of your product, the mass market appeal, and the potential longevity, you also need to show them that representing you will be worthwhile from a financial perspective. To prepare a pitch for a distributor, you should use the same guidelines given in Part Two for pitching to a buyer as each distribution business has their own set of buyers.

In other words, a distributor will want to be confident that, eventually, they will be selling large enough quantities of your products so that the financial return will be worth the work.

Wholesaler case study

- **Name**: Kate Shrubb
- **Company**: Babybase Wholesale
- **Position**: Managing Director

What is the benefit of using a wholesaler?

The idea of a wholesaler is that the retailer can buy a selection of products made by different companies in one easy transaction and they can have singles rather than boxed quantities. It works especially well for companies who only have a couple of products but we also deal with the big firms too.

How should sellers make initial contact?

The first contact is usually by telephone or by email. On the phone I get very fed up with the people who pretend to know me so they can get through my secretary! In both cases I really don't like being called by my first name by people I have never met. I am quite old fashioned and like a courteous and not too pushy approach. I usually ask people to send me details plus a sample if that is feasible so that I can see if it is the kind of product we would be interested in. If I am interested I will get back to people – they don't need to nag. Another thing I don't like these days is people who send me lots of brochures by email so I either have to strain my eyes looking at them online or use ink printing them off.

What happens next?

If I want to proceed I will ask people to come and see me. I do expect them to have done a little bit of homework and know how wholesalers work in advance. They should have in mind the kind of discount they can afford to give us together with the size of order that is necessary to get that discount. Things that are important to me are stock availability, time from order to delivery, payment terms, etc., and I would hope that some thought has been given to these before the meeting.

What format does the meeting take?

When I meet people I like to talk to them, not watch PowerPoint presentations. I want to do business with people I like so it is important for me to talk to people and get to know them as well as their products. If I want to see samples I will ask for them, but I don't like people to bring hundreds of items. If I am interested in one or two, I will be likely to look at more in the future.

Although I am in the meeting to listen to the pitcher they need to also do lots of listening. Every customer is different and if you treat them all the same, you won't make a good impression. Manufacturers who treat me in the same way that they treat Argos don't sell to me – mainly because I don't speak that language!

What is the best piece of advice you could give?

First form the relationship and then sell the product.

Retailer case study

- **Name** – Cara Sayer
- **Company** – SnoozeShade (Really Simple Ideas Ltd)
- **Position** – Managing Director
- **Email** – info@snoozeshade.com

What, in your opinion, is the best way to get the name of the correct buyer for your product?

I met my first retailers by exhibiting at the Baby Products Association Show. This meant I had personally met them when I followed up after the show. I also chatted to other exhibitors who were happy to share their contacts. Trade shows are vital in this way and enable you to build relationships with key buyers.

Retailers are a shy lot and the biggest mistake I see people making is to exhibit at a show and then stand quietly behind their stand. If you are a new product it is unlikely anyone will hunt you out so you have to chat to visitors to find out who they are and what the purpose of their visit is. If they are relevant to you and your product, briefly explain your product's USP (unique selling point) and ask if they'd like to know more. Try to get their card and follow up after the event.

Have you found any particular method that gets the attention of buyers via phone or email?

I haven't found calling to be the best way of initiating a conversation. Buyers must be inundated with products so my top tip would be to treat a buyer like a PR treats a journalist looking for a story. Sell them your product in a short and punchy style. Start off with why it's new, what reception it's had from media and consumers and tell them what the RRP is.

Don't go in with offers on price as it's immaterial if they don't like the product. Don't be afraid of saying who else is stocking your product and if you have any sales data then use it.

Were you asked any questions that you weren't prepared for?

Not really. I tried to ensure that I had as much information as possible so I could answer any questions. If I didn't know the answer to a certain question while I was meeting with buyers I would tell them so and then go away to find out. I'd be sure to get back to them promptly with the relevant information.

Did you do anything to make your pitch stand out?

I ensured they knew that my marketing background was a strong asset to the brand. I had already secured some coverage for SnoozeShade's launch so it was nice to be able to say that if they were signed up they would be listed as a stockist from launch when I was expecting media attention. As time has gone by I have updated retailers with award wins and press coverage.

Was there a particular part of the pitching process that you found extremely difficult? If yes, what solution did you find?

Price negotiations are the hardest part when you start off. When I started I made a few mistakes with pricing but was very lucky and was able to amend them. Make sure you've worked out your pricing so you know it inside out and don't go too low from the beginning.

Most major retailers expect 50% margin on the price they pay you so if you are only going to make a tiny margin then look at how you can get your costs down to increase your share. Have a standard trade price that you are happy with, e.g. 35-40% margin, and present that as a first offer. Big chains often won't deal with a one-product business so you may need to appoint a distributor – check your pricing can afford that additional cost.

What is the most useful advice you could give for pitching a product to a retailer?

Research, research, research and know your market. Research the retailer, who they are, where are they based, whether they operate online, in stores or both and how long they have been going. Also research your competition. Know them inside out and keep your eyes peeled for competitive products as they launch. Retailers will always ask you about them so show you are an expert in your field. Check out which retailers your competitor's products are stocked at.

Be strategic with your pricing structure and production capabilities. Can you produce enough products if you get a big order? Can you afford to have any third parties involved, e.g. if you get talking to a retail chain they may not deal with individual companies and you may need to get a distributor involved, which will require you to relinquish some margin.

Chapter 3

Pre-pitch Research

Researching your target retailer

Before you approach any retailer to pitch them your product you should research the retailer and their buying department, if they have one. It would be unprofessional and a waste of your time to complete a full pitch to a retailer only for the buyer to point out that your product does not meet their target demographic and that in fact they don't even have a department that the product could fit into.

You need to know – and the retailer you are pitching needs to be convinced – that the consumer coming into the store, flicking through their catalogue or browsing their website would associate your product with that retailer. You need to know whether or not your target retailer stocks any other similar products and you need to know how well those products sell.

Use business reports

The best way to get your hands on really in-depth information is to look at the retailer's annual business report for the previous year. This is freely available online using their respective corporate website. Alternatively, you can call their head office and ask for a copy of the report, which they can send by post.

These reports contain a vast array of information, from their pension contributions to growth, in particular product lines and profits relating to certain sectors. They can be fairly long-winded but it's worth taking the time to read through them fully because there are several little gems hidden within each. For example, whilst glancing through the 2009/10 report for John Lewis, I noticed the following:

We saw total sales growth of 9% in Fashion, 4% in EHT (electrical and home technology) and 3% in Home, and in all categories we increased market share.

We continued to grow strongly with 25 new stores in the UK, including three new convenience format stores, together these openings added 390,000 sq ft of new selling space. Our online service Waitrose Deliver is now available in 129 branches. This is growing in parallel with Ocado, with whom Waitrose has a supply relationship. During the year we entered into a strategic partnership with Welcome Break and commenced trials with Shell, further extending the reach of the Waitrose brand.

This kind of knowledge, if placed correctly within a pitch or presentation, will show the buyer how much research you have done and will also help you with your case. A pitch to John Lewis could mention that a new product would be perfectly placed in the store's home category. Considering that John Lewis had a 3% growth rate in that category, you could suggest that they could probably expect a rise for the 2010/11 year as well, as economic conditions improve. You could express that this would be the perfect time to showcase a new product in the home category.

Visit the store and talk to staff

If you can't find the information that you need in the annual report and you're thinking of pitching a new piece of exercise equipment to John Lewis, for example, pay a visit to your local store. Take a look at the items already stocked in that department. Have a little fun whilst you're there and play private detective.

Speak to a member of staff that works in that department and ask questions about the product that is most like yours – you could ask whether they sell many of them. Have they stocked the product for long? Do they stock it in many of their other stores?

If there is nothing like your product already there you need to be a little more subtle. Say you are looking for a product that can do A, B and C, and do they stock anything like it? If not, try and ascertain why not. It could be because there is nothing like that on the market or it could be because there is no demand for a product that can do those things. If this is carried out as more of a conversation rather than an interrogation the sales person will assume that you are a cautious buyer rather than a potential supplier.

Talk to a store's other suppliers

You can further investigate prospective retailers by asking other suppliers about them. If you don't know any of their current suppliers personally, again, take a look around one of their stores and identify products that they have already listed that fall within your category. Follow this up with a little research on the internet and before you know it you'll have the name and number of a supplier.

Now be brave and call them. Be completely honest and explain why you're calling. Ask for advice or, if you're feeling particularly cheeky, after a little chat, why not ask about the possibility of an introduction. Obviously this is not something you should do with a business that carries any products similar to yours as they would see you as competition.

Remember that the worst thing that can happen when you are making approaches like this is that someone will say no. That's it.

Visit other suppliers at trade shows

Try investigating relevant trade shows. If there is a show coming up, take a look at the organiser's website. They will always have a list of exhibitors with links to their websites. Take a look through the stockists on each exhibitor's website and try to get the details of three or four that are currently supplying to your target store. Armed with this information, head off to the show and during the quiet periods approach the exhibitor. Once more, be completely honest with your reason for approaching them – say you are looking for advice on getting your products stocked with certain stores.

Buying departments and buyers

A buying department is a department within a company that handles all purchasing of wholesale goods. Within the department there are a series of buyers who make the buying decisions on behalf of the company. They know all about their demographic and know what will and won't appeal to them. Their job is to find the best new products that appear on the market and get them stocked at the best possible price.

If the store covers more than one industry you may find that the buyers are broken down into categories, i.e. homeware, fashion, etc.

The key is to find out who the most appropriate buyer for your industry is and to make contact with them or their assistant.

Start with research

In any major retailer you can be assured that there are multiple buyers for each department. Take a look at Argos, for example. This is a huge business that sells a vast array of products. They have in excess of 30 senior buyers all covering different product areas and more than 60 buying assistants and merchandise executives. To establish how big your target buying department is or to find out which section of the buying department you need to be targeting, you should call the head office, the phone number of which should be readily available on the internet.

You then need to establish how many buying departments would be interested in your product. Usually it would only be one but occasionally a product could fall under two or more categories. Think of a vacuum cleaner, for example. This could quite easily be categorised under *appliances* and *electrical items*, and some department stores would have buyers for each.

Take a look at a retailer's existing product ranges and establish which your product best falls under. If you can see more than one or two, make a shortlist and then look a little deeper into what each range carries. It should be easy enough to find the right department for your product to slot into. However, if you're struggling then call the business and ask which department they think your product would fall under. Perhaps ask for their marketing department, who should be able to give you a breakdown of the buying department structure.

Contacting the buying department

Now that you have some basic information about a retailer's buying departments you need to establish which buyer is the most appropriate one for you to speak to. The easiest way to do this is to simply ask.

Most head office switchboards will either tell you the name of a buying executive or, if you're really lucky, the head of buying for the department you are trying to contact. If they say that it is against business policy to give out names, simply request that you be transferred to that specific department and ask whoever answers the phone. More often than not that person will give you a contact name. If they aren't quite as forthcoming as you'd like, ask them for the normal procedure used when trying to make contact with their buyers.

It's highly likely that you will initially speak to a buying assistant or executive. Don't let this phase you. Their job is to field calls away from the head buyers and buying directors. If you can get the attention of this individual you are on your way to an appointment.

If you do get through to a buying assistant, bear in mind that they will be the one that initially presents your product to the people with the spending power – the head buyers – and if they aren't convinced then they will not be able or willing to convince other members of the buying team.

Use this opportunity to practice your pitch. Give a mini pitch to the assistant ensuring you include:

- The USP (unique selling point) of your product.
- At least two features and the benefit to the consumer.
- Brief details of any research evidence you have.

At this point in time you don't really want to be talking about pricing in any detail. If asked, simply explain that you have a pricing structure in place so it depends on the number of units that are ordered.

Once you are confident that you have clearly expressed the benefit of stocking your item ask if they would like to see a sample to help them demonstrate it to the person who makes the buying decisions. Before ending the call, be sure to ask the following two questions:

- Is there any aspect of the product that you are unsure of or don't understand?
- When will you be speaking to the other members of the buying team and when should I call you back?
- Get their direct contact details so that you can get in touch with them again if you have to.

This will give you the chance to get rid of any doubts they may have and also give you an indication of when you should follow up.

Speaking to the head buyer

The dream scenario is the one where you are given the details of the head buyer straightaway – you are then in a good position. Before you speak to them, have a little run through in your head of what you plan to say and how you plan to introduce your business.

A great tip is to act as if the buyer should already be aware of who you are. This does not mean you should take an attitude of "Don't you know who I am!" Rather, when you do get through to a buyer, don't introduce yourself by saying:

Hi, I'm Helen from a business called The Fresh Business and I would like to tell you about our new product.

You should introduce yourself by saying:

Hi, this is Helen from The Fresh Business and I want to let you know about our fantastic new product!

Notice the difference. The first statement is a little uncertain whereas the second is full of confidence and surety.

The tone of your voice and the way in which you introduce yourself are imperative when it comes to grabbing a buyer's attention. Think about it for a second. How many calls and emails do you think they receive on a weekly basis from people who are launching the next big thing? Hundreds, that's how many!

You need to sound completely confident and self-assured but not arrogant. If there is any weakness in your voice it gives the impression that you aren't entirely ready to be making this call, which in turn gives the buyer the impression that your product and your business aren't entirely worthy of their shelf space. Confidence when introducing yourself shows that you have confidence in your business and product.

Be prepared for your initial call to be a short one. Buyers are extremely busy and don't necessarily have the time to get into full blown pitches over the phone. This is why your call has to make an impression. You will more than likely be asked to send additional information by email or, if they are really interested, they may request a sample to be sent directly to them.

Before ending the call, ask when you should call back to discuss your product in further detail. If possible try to pinpoint a specific date and time. If you do arrange a time for a future call be sure to follow up when you have promised to. Failure to do so would make a very bad impression.

Contacting buyers by email

Introductions via email can be successful; in fact there are some buyers who prefer this method to telephone calls. My only issue with email introductions is that you are never sure whether or not your email has been read or deleted. Adding a 'read request' to an email will often annoy the recipient so this is definitely not something I would recommend. If you try to make introductions via email, I would suggest writing a message along the lines of the following:

Template email for contacting a buyer

Dear Mr Buyer,

I am writing to make you aware of a brand new product we are about to launch onto the market. The Fresh Co are a newly established business specialising in home perfume and we have developed a new product that I feel suits your target market perfectly and I am sure that you will agree.

Freshen-Up is absolutely unique and I would love the opportunity to discuss further the possibilities of working with your business.

[Freshen-up has been designed with the ... market in mind and as they too are your target market, I feel this product could enhance your existing range.]

I have attached some images and additional information/short presentation for you to take a look at and I will call you on Tuesday 22nd at 10:30am to discuss in further detail.

If this time or date is inconvenient for you please do get in touch to re-schedule.

Kindest regards,

Helen Inventor

This email is short, relevant and straight to the point. In my experience buyers do not have the time to be reading long introductions; they simply want to know who you are, what you are selling and whether or not it's right for their store. By keeping the email to the point you are giving them the opportunity to make these decisions without feeling harassed.

If you are able to put together a brief PowerPoint or PDF presentation to show some of the key statistics or figures unearthed during your market research, then do so. Don't forget to include some eye-catching images or graphics of both the product and the packaging.

Adding the follow-up call details to the end of the email makes the buyer aware that they have a certain amount of time to look through it and this should make it more of a priority for them, whilst showing that you mean business. If you receive no response, assume that the buyer is happy with the date and time stated and follow up as planned. If you encounter any problems getting through to the buyer, you can now state that the person you are calling is expecting your call. After all, you have told them you would be in touch at that specific time.

I know a few individuals who have sold to major retailers by using email alone. They have received purchase orders never having once spoken to anyone, but just following a series of emails. The trick is in establishing which method your buyer prefers. This might not be obvious but if you are struggling to get through via phone then email may be a better option.

What to do if you're struggling to contact buyers

If you have tried everything you can think of to get names, numbers and email addresses and you're still having no luck, here are a few tips that may just lead to a breakthrough:

Google phrases such as "head buyer at store name". Quite often you will find articles from trade journals that have quotes from named buyers.

Search for the term "buyer" and the store name on social networking site LinkedIn. You may not always find the name of the buyer you need but you may be able to connect with a colleague who could potentially assist you.

If the switchboard is definitely not going to put you through, try dialling the number again but alter the last digit. With any luck you will get through to an alternative department where somebody may just put you through or even give you a direct line.

Quite often, email addresses take the standard form of **firstname.lastname@businesswebsite.co.uk** and it's always worth a try. If it bounces back, call the switchboard operator and say you think you may have taken down a person's email address incorrectly as your message had bounced back . Ask if they would they please provide you with the correct one. This works because it gives the impression that you have spoken previously to someone without you having to say so.

Visit a store and ask to speak to a manager

If all else fails and you are still without the name and number of the buyer you need to talk to, head to your local branch of your target retailer and ask to speak to the manager. Be completely honest with them, explain what you are trying to achieve and show them your product. Whilst it's not their job to do any buying you can at least ask for their opinion.

Ask if they would be willing to find out the name of the contact that you require and you could even go as far as asking them to send an introductory email on your behalf. Let's face it, the worst that can happen is that they say no – you will have lost precisely nothing.

Trade fairs

Exhibiting your product at appropriate trade fairs is a good way to get the attention of a buyer. Trade fairs are events that are designed to showcase and highlight new and existing products, and are attended by industry professional and buyers from all over the country (or maybe even further afield).

The opportunities that can come from exhibiting at a trade fair are wide ranging. Not only do you get the opportunity to meet and speak directly to buyers but you can also gauge their initial reaction to your product. If you are planning to exhibit at one of these events it is very wise to introduce yourself to a handful of your target buyers via phone or email in the two or three weeks prior to the event taking place.

You can then use the opportunity to let them know that you will be attending the event and that should they also be attending you would be grateful to speak to them for five minutes, their schedule permitting. This means that they don't have to go out of their way to meet you or arrange meetings – they can simply wander over to your stand at a time that is convenient to them and assess your product first hand.

Be aware that trade fairs can be very expensive to exhibit at. Even the smallest of stands can cost you over £2000, which for a start-up business is a huge outlay. If you can't yet afford to exhibit at a fair you still need to be seen there, so go along armed with a product sample (if it's practical to carry it around) and plenty of business cards. Everyone at trade shows wears a name badge, so if you keep your eyes peeled you may be lucky enough to spot the particular buyers you've been trying to get hold of. It is also worth having your own name badge and logo. This shows that you are a professional whilst also helping to raise awareness of your company.

If you are exhibiting, simply sitting and waiting for a buyer to approach you will not always work – apart from not giving a positive image, your buyer may have been held up or waylaid so you need to be proactive. Don't be shy about walking up to someone in a crowd, sticking your hand out and introducing yourself. This kind of self-confidence will make you more attractive to those with the buying power. It shows that you are willing to take risks when it comes to moving your business forward. Who wants to do business with someone that is always that little bit too timid to ask the right questions or get in front of the right people?

At trade shows make a point of handing out your business card and introducing yourself to exhibitors with products that are relevant to your industry. At some point they may well be speaking to a buyer that you would like to make contact with. By making friends with others that are already dealing with buyers it gets you one step closer to the decision maker.

People in the same position as you will be more willing to help you than you may think because making contact with you helps to build their network as well as yours. Don't forget you may one day have a buying contact that they would like to be introduced to, so the gesture may be reciprocated.

Case study: trying something different

Neil Westwood – Magic Whiteboard

Magic Whiteboard is the tear-off whiteboard made famous when Neil and Laura Westwood appeared on *Dragons' Den* on the BBC. Neil tried something a little different to get noticed by a buyer. He says:

> We had tried for a long time to get in front of buyers at Staples. Our product was an obvious choice for them but for some reason they were unreceptive to any kind of introduction we attempted. I decided one day to drive to their head office and try to see a buyer in person but as I sat in the car thinking about the best way to approach them something caught my eye.
>
> Across the road from their office was a huge billboard and an idea started to form in my head. I took out advertising space on the billboard and promptly had a huge advert displayed for Magic Whiteboard knowing that the MD would see it every day on his way to work. Within a week I had a phone call from

the managing director of Staples requesting that I meet with his buying director and the rest is history!

It was a long shot and I knew full well that I may never achieve anything by using this tactic but it was a risk I'm glad I took. I believe I would still be struggling to get in front of their buyers had I not carried out my plan and whilst I know it was slightly cheeky, it had the desired results and we are now stocked in Staples stores nationwide.

I would always advise others who are struggling to get in front of buyers to be creative. Try and think of a way that will really make them sit up and listen. It won't always work but you have nothing to lose and everything to gain.

Retailer case study

- **Name** – Max Wiseberg
- **Company** – Haymax
- **Email** – info@haymax.biz

I have followed a slightly unusual approach to pitching to major retailers. Most people say it's imperative to meet with the buyers. On the basis that most buyers are relatively young and have been brought up in the digital age, I believe they are very comfortable with forming relationships without face-to-face meetings. They are also extremely busy – if they were to meet everyone who pitched to them, they would not have time to do their job.

Therefore, my strategy is to write a fairly brief covering email and attach a one-page document containing the advantages of listing our product in bullet point format. When writing the email put yourself in the buyer's position and think about what will get their interest.

I then follow this up with phone calls until I get through to them. When I get through to voicemail I leave a very brief message signposting me, my product and the email. I would not ask them to ring back, although I would leave my phone number, spoken slowly and clearly so they have time to write it down while listening to the message.

By conducting my relationship with them in this way, I can talk to them and pitch my product in a matter of minutes. This way they do not have to spend time arranging an appointment. Just as important, most people seem to assume that a meeting will take around an hour, including pleasantries around introductions, walking to the meeting room, getting drinks, all this before you've talked about the products. Then you'll go over the stuff you've already talked about by email and on the phone. How much more attractive is it to the buyer to deal with all of this over the phone in a few minutes?

My successful pitches to Waitrose, Superdrug, Tesco, and to several wholesalers were all done without a meeting, although I did meet the Waitrose buyer at a couple of trade shows at which we exhibited. This was after he had decided to list us and was at his convenience while he was seeing several others.

We are now listed in Tesco, Boots (and their wholesaler to independents – Alliance Pharmacy), Asda, Lloyds pharmacy, Waitrose and many other smaller chains and independents.

Part Two

Meeting With Buyers

If you have followed the steps laid out in Part One you will have put in place the necessary foundations on which to build a successful pitch to buyers. You will also hopefully have had some success in contacting buyers and arranging meetings with them, at which you will make your pitch.

In Part Two we look at meeting with buyers – including how to make a good pitch – and also at haggling and exclusivity deals.

Chapter 4

Presenting Your Product

Product knowledge

Before you attempt to pitch your product to any retail buyers you should know anything and everything there is to know about it. You should be a walking encyclopaedia, with knowledge of:

- How the product is made.
- Where it's made.
- What materials are used.
- The length of time it takes to manufacture.
- If manufactured abroad, the length of time it takes to arrive in the UK.

Whether it complies with any relevant UK safety standards, etc.

You need to know all of this information so that no matter what questions a buyer asks, you have the answer implanted firmly in your brain. This will show that you are professional, organised and know what you are talking about, and it also shows that you are ready to introduce your product to the mass market.

You should also know all about the store you are pitching to. If you have knowledge regarding their buying cycles, their current product range and where your product would fit into their catalogues and onto their store shelves this shows that you are genuinely interested in being in business with them.

This information can be discovered by asking the company itself. Call and request details on their buying cycles or explain that you would like to approach a buyer with your products but don't want to waste their time and would appreciate knowing when's best in the year to make your introduction. You should find that the receptionists and assistants are willing to supply you with the answers. After all, it makes their lives a little easier too.

Unexpected questions

Even if you have researched everything thoroughly there is still a chance that you will be caught unawares by a question you don't have the answer to. Should this happen, don't try to be clever and simply skirt around the answer or make something up. It is better to say that you are unsure but will confirm the answer in an email the following day than to bluff your way through.

Buyers do understand that this can be a nerve-wracking time for you and that this is a big deal for your business, so they should be understanding if nervousness kicks in. By being honest and admitting that you are unsure of an answer it shows the buyer that you can be trusted. Honesty really is the best policy.

Presentation

When it comes to the presentation itself, you don't need to have big screens, slideshows and fancy special effects. The buyer wants to know facts so the key is to get the appropriate information across in a professional way.

Structure of a pitch

This may sound obvious, but your presentation needs to be split into three parts:

1. Introduction.
2. Add detail and demonstrate your product.
3. Conclusion.

First you should introduce yourself, your business and the product. Then tell your story, give more in-depth product detail, market research and any other relevant information. Finally, end with your concluding summary and close.

1. Introduction

Open your pitch by introducing yourself to the buyer. Make them aware of who you are and what your background is. Then tell them about your business as a whole. They want to know about your achievements to date, your plans for the future and your ultimate vision. All of this demonstrates your passion and commitment to your business and helps them to understand how you operate.

They will already know something about the product you are pitching to them as you will have introduced it by telephone or email, so you need to present it in a new, fresh and exciting way. Tell them about any accolades or awards you have won, tell them about any industry recognised recommendations you have received. Most important of all, whatever you tell them, keep it brief and leave them wanting more. Though not at the risk of not covering enough ground.

2. Add detail and demonstrate your product

Now you can build more detail into your presentation. Start off by explaining the thinking behind your product and use this opportunity to tell your story. What gave you the idea? What problem does your product solve? How will the product make consumers' lives easier or better?

Give a full demonstration of your product and if feasible get the buyer involved by asking them to use it too. Here is where you need to explain every feature and show the benefit to the consumer. Use the research you have done to make it relevant and pull out the statistics and feedback you established during your market research. Remember to bring any additional props you may need with you.

Match the product to the business by making a statement with a confirmatory ending, such as "...and that's why it would fit well within your homeware department." This helps the buyer to commit throughout the process and makes the decision making somewhat easier at the end.

When preparing this part of your presentation you need to think about and cover each of the following points:

- What competition do you have and why are you better?
- How does the price compare to your competition?
- What is the target market for your product and how does it fit with the retailer's consumers?
- Where would it fit in the retailer's store?
- What other retailers are stocking your product?
- Do you have any kind of patent or patent pending?
- Do you offer any kind of warranty?
- Does your product meet all the required safety standards?
- What is your RRP?
- How is your product packaged?
- What is the unique selling point (USP)?
- What marketing and promotions do you have planned for the next 12 months?
- How many units have you sold to date?
- What is your shipping time?
- How will you physically get the products to them?

Covering all of these points during your presentation should leave the buyer with less reason for objection, which will mean fewer reasons not to buy.

3. Conclusion

The conclusion of your presentation is where you start talking price. Be confident when explaining your unit price and any additional pricing structure you have in place. Make sure you state the margin the retailer will receive when the product is sold at the RRP.

Try to get some form of commitment from the buyer at this point. Whilst it's unlikely you will receive an order on the spot you should aim to get some idea of if and when they will be placing an order. If the buyer is not interested in listing your product, rest assured you will be told pretty much instantly so if you leave without an answer, this should be seen as a positive.

Practice before you pitch

Make sure you know your pitch inside out. Practice, practice and practice some more. Don't be shy about taking some notes with you – the person you are pitching to will have seen it all before and knowing how much information you are expected to get across they will more than likely expect you to have a few bullet points written down somewhere. If you do take notes, be sure that you have them in the correct order before entering a pitch environment.

During the pitch

At the beginning of the meeting

When you enter the meeting room be sure to walk in with confidence, shake hands, hold eye contact and greet each buyer individually, then take a seat where instructed to. Buyers are busy so don't expect them to make small talk with you. They want to see what you have and they want you to tell them why they should stock it.

Be clear, concise, confident and show belief

When delivering your pitch you need to be clear, concise and confident. You need to show belief in your product because if you are convinced by it others will be convinced too.

Engage your audience with questions

Try not to simply talk at those in front of you. Try to tell a story and keep your audience engaged by getting their agreement along the way. Whilst demonstrating how your product works say things like "Do you see how that works?"

When going through your market research try fitting in a little line such as "So you can see that there is already a market for this product, can't you?" This will ensure that the buyer has to keep listening and it will keep them focussed.

Try to remain in control throughout

There may be times that a buyer interrupts your presentation to ask questions about a particular feature or a point that you have raised. This is a positive because your pitch should ideally be an interactive conversation with the buyers, rather than a monologue delivered by you. Answer any questions to the best of your ability and then continue with your pitch. Should this situation arise be sure never to restart your presentation by using the phrase "As I was saying…". This could be construed as rude and may turn the listeners against you.

Buyers are human too

Buyers, like consumers, buy from the heart. They will be thinking about whether or not they would buy your product, whether they would use it, or whether they can think of anyone else who would. Of course, they are always thinking about the business side of things but it's human nature to look at products from an emotional point of view. Use this to your advantage and if possible try to get the buyers to tell you what aspects of your product they really like. This will also help you gauge which step to take next, as once you know their favourite aspects you can start highlighting the benefits of other aspects of your product that the buyer has so far failed to appreciate.

Examples of your product and visual aids

Make your presentation interesting by bringing along samples that the buyers can look at whilst you pitch. Encourage them to thoroughly examine and play with the item. Getting them involved will also help to ease any tension or nervousness on your part.

If you have any brochures ensure you take those along too. Visual aids are a huge bonus when you are presenting to people as they add substance to your pitch and also give the buyers something to take away with them so that you and your products stay fresh in their minds.

Provide a pitch summary

Compile a brief summary of your pitch that you can hand out, and be sure to include all of the key facts and figures that you have researched. These will more than likely be passed around various members of the department so you need to ensure that they are completely up to date. These pieces of literature will represent you and your brand when you're not there so they should be prepared to a very high standard. Also ensure it includes your full contact details.

Buyer case study

- **Name** – Pamela Johnson
- **Company** – Bensons for Beds
- **Position** – Buyer

Is there any easy way to get a buyer's attention via phone or email?

In the first instance a short phone call, followed by information from the potential supplier (if the product is appropriate). This is best sent by email as then it will always be readily available.

What are the most common mistakes made when individuals pitch products for sale?

Long introductory phone calls – the buyer may well be busy and the product may not be appropriate for your business.

Constant hassling – if a product is truly suitable for a buyer, they will not ignore it, however timing is often critical. For instance, in November and December each year we are extremely busy preparing for the January sale, therefore this leaves little or no opportunity to see suppliers during this period and even less opportunity to introduce products.

Give your best price first time – this builds up trust and saves everyone a lot of time. If this method is used from day one everyone knows where they stand and a relationship of trust can be built up.

In retail most buyers are tied up on a Monday reviewing the previous week's trade, so often do not wish to be contacted on this day of the week.

Are there any questions you tend to always ask?

- What is the lead time?
- Is there a guarantee?
- What are the minimum order quantities?
- Can you offer exclusivity?

What makes a great pitch?

It is very important that you feel the person pitching to you has a good overview of your business. It is frustrating when someone visits you to make a pitch and they have never visited one of our retail outlets.

Integrity always shines through.

A prompt follow-up, preferably by email, speeds up the product introduction process and assists the buyer greatly. A great pitch and poor follow-up is a cardinal sin.

Short and sharp.

Is there a particular past pitch that sticks out in your memory? If yes, why?

One for the wrong reasons – A supplier came to discuss a new, upgraded product to one that we were currently running and did not bring a sample of the current one or the proposed new one. This is memorable because the appointment was a complete waste of time.

One for good reasons – A pitch on a new children's collection by a new supplier who had a great understanding of our retail business, had visited a number of our stores and those of our competitors, so they understood the marketplace. They gave a very short, punchy pitch and followed up very promptly on product amendments. This was probably the quickest product launch I've seen, and the product sells well.

If you could give one piece of advice about pitching a product to a retailer what would it be?

Never lie or bluff. If you don't know then say you will find out later. Finally, don't hassle the buyer.

Chapter 5

Making Deals with Buyers

Haggling, large order discounts and exclusivity are just a few of the terms you may encounter when it comes to interacting with buyers. Make sure you're prepared to deal with every scenario.

Haggling

When you go enter into a pitching situation, be it over the phone, via email or face to face, you should always be aware of your price limits and be prepared to be haggled. Everyone has an ideal wholesale price for their product but quite often that price isn't realised when sold to retailers. It is part of a buyer's job to ensure they get a great product at a good price, so they will almost certainly try to haggle you down.

In your head you may know, for example, that your ideal wholesale price is £9.87 per unit but you may also be aware that you could sell directly to a retailer at £8.43 per unit and still make a healthy profit. Don't be frightened to go straight in at the higher price – most buyers will be fully prepared to try to haggle the price down.

For instance, if a buyer comes back to you following your pitch saying that they like your product and believe they have a market for it but would like to trial it to begin with, explain that you understand the position and would be happy to negotiate a slightly better price on long-term deals, but initial trial orders will need to be at a price close to the list price. If they like your product enough, they will not be put off by this and will probably appreciate your direct response.

Don't be tempted to go in with over-inflated prices so that you can follow up with huge discounts. Buyers will see through this immediately and it will damage your credibility. They may also assume that you are pricing yourself out of the market and reason that they cannot do business with you on that basis.

Have a pricing structure in place

A good way to encourage larger orders is to have a pricing structure in place from the start. Table 5.1 provides an example of such a structure.

Table 5.1 – example pricing structure

Number of units	Price per unit (£)
Up to 499	9.87
500 – 999	9.35
1000 - 4999	8.99
5000 +	8.25

It is also worth putting some thought into delivery charges. Rather than offering free delivery on larger orders and charging for smaller ones, set a small standard delivery charge regardless of quantity. Bear in mind that if you're shipping pallets of goods this is expensive so if at all possible try to get the buyer to cover some of the cost by adding a small delivery charge.

If the delivery charges look like being a deal breaker, then you should offer to waive them. Most companies will expect some kind of shipping or handling fee but it's not worth losing an order for the sake of a few pounds.

Be organised when using different rates

Keep a file of all of your retailers, both confirmed and pending. Keep detailed notes of all conversations including dates and times and a printed copy of all emails that have gone back and forth. Before making any phone calls to enquire about new orders or a general catch up to see how the product is getting on, take a look through your notes. This way you will always know exactly where you stand with each reseller, you will always know the state of play and more importantly you will always know the pricing structure that you have agreed with them.

Long term you will may find that you have different rates for different resellers. This is where organisation becomes important. Picture the scene – you get an email from Buyer A, who you have been dealing with for 18 months, placing an order for 100 units. You have an agreed price of £9.21 per unit with them, but in your rush to get the buyer to raise the purchase order, you accidentally send a reply stating a price of your agreed price with Buyer B of £9.03 per unit. This is great news for Buyer A, as they have an extra discount of 18p per unit, but this is not so great for you.

This kind of error would more than likely lead to you having to reduce your price for Buyer A to £9.03 for all future orders, meaning a drop in profits. If you confuse one retailer's wholesale price with another's you may lose money, but the worst case scenario is potentially a lost contract.

Double check every agreement, invoice or email confirmation before sending. An extra five minutes added to your processing time will not result in a lost order but rushing and making errors will give a bad impression and, at worst, lose you a retailer.

Buyer case study

- **Company** – Perfectly Happy People Ltd
- **Position** – Buyer

Is there any easy way to get a buyer's attention via phone or email?

Try phoning first then try sending an email – be polite and keep communication brief. Buyers don't have much free time.

Are there any generic questions that you tend to ask?

- Do you have a patent?
- Do you have many competitors?
- Is the price point realistic?
- Has it been tested?
- Where is it made?

What makes a great pitch?

Keep it short! Provide a one-page snapshot with five bullet points and a great image, plus a website so buyers can check for more detail during discussion.

If you could give one piece of advice about pitching a product to a retailer what would it be?

Choose your timing carefully. Monday at 10am is not a good idea but on Wednesday afternoon the buyer will more likely have time to listen.

Exclusivity deals

Exclusivity basically means allowing one retailer to stock a particular product from your range exclusively for a set period of time, disallowing you from selling to any other retailer within that time frame. These deals can be great if they are agreed with the right retailers and with the right terms and conditions.

An exclusivity deal is restrictive in a sense, but overall it is very positive. Think of it this way. If a business offers you an order on an exclusivity basis it means they are very excited about your product. They can see that there is a market for it and that it has the potential to sell well. By offering exclusivity, they are showing that they have belief in your product.

If this proposition is put to you it will usually be accompanied by a large order, which should add weight to the offer and encourage you to agree. However, before making any decisions there are things you need to consider:

Whilst exclusivity restricts you from having your product listed with any other retailers it doesn't stop you from approaching other buyers with a view to having your product stocked once your current agreement expires. This means that you can continue contacting potential retailers with the knowledge that you have an income in the meantime. With any luck this will also mean that once the exclusivity deal has ended you will have a queue of retailers ready and waiting with purchase orders at the ready.

If you have a range of products and the retailer is looking to place an order which includes more than one product line, agree exclusivity on a particular product rather than the whole range – this is a good compromise and still allows you the freedom to approach additional retailers. The retailer still has the knowledge that they will be the only business stocking a specific product for the period of the deal.

If your product comes in different colours, styles or fabrics you might be able to offer an exclusive design and open up the chance to sell different designs to other groups. You could also offer exclusive branding of your product for certain retailers.

Most exclusivity deals are for a period of 12 months. You could try to arrange a six-month deal as a trial and, dependent upon the success and volume of orders, review it at the end.

These tactics may not always work but it's worth putting the suggestions to buyers. At the point the subject of an exclusivity deal is broached you know that the retailer is extremely interested, which gives you the chance to take a little control.

Exclusivity is a very important arrangement and you need to take it very seriously without letting the initial excitement cloud your judgement. Be sure that any agreements benefit not only the retailer but your business also.

Buyer case study

- **Name** – Jo O'Brien
- **Company** – Surfdome
- **Position** – Head of Buying
- **Email** – jo.obrien@surfdome.com

Is there an easy way to get a buyer's attention via phone or email?

Our buyers are usually out at appointments and focused on getting orders in during the season, so it is best to try and catch them out of the buying season. A great way to catch their attention is to provide a PowerPoint presentation or PDF which catches the eye. The presentation needs to be succinct yet exciting so that the buyer can relate to the product straight away.

Always try to follow up with a phone call on the same day as an email or presentation is sent. If you really want to get your product in front of a buyer send a couple of samples by post, as this often results in the products being passed around the buying office and begins the internal marketing of your brand within the organisation you are pitching to.

The buyer needs enough information to warrant making an appointment such as brand demographics, marketing/advertising images or videos. They need a taster of retail prices, margins and commercial terms so they can determine if it will fit into the current brand and product mix. The buyer wants to see brands that will fill a gap in their existing range.

What are the most common mistakes made when individuals pitch products for sale?

- A lack of research on the business being pitched to.
- A lack of awareness of the current brand mix or product mix.
- The product isn't priced correctly to enter the market.
- Trying to enter the market in the wrong season.
- Arriving at the pitch meeting without catalogues, samples or tools to present with.

The perfect pitcher should have all of the relevant facts and figures handy to support their pitch. Facts such as year-on-year growth for their brand or product, volume of their business and planned marketing spend are important.

Are there any questions that you always ask?

- What are margins?
- What are the commercial trading terms, including credit terms, mark-down allowance, discount structure? These are key so that the product is profitable for the retailer. For an online retailer it is also very important that the market you are going into isn't too price sensitive and there is room for the retailer to come into the market place.
- What marketing has been done already and what will be done in the future to promote the brand/product?
- What is the buying cycle?
- Do you have lifestyle images, video, or product shots we can use?
- Are we able to sell through third-party websites? Who are you supplying the product to and how are you going to protect your pricing strategy? Do we need trading permission to advertise through Google PPC?
- What are your best sellers, which products will you have risk stock on, and do you provide option orders?
- Do you provide sale or return, consignment or drop ship delivery options?

- Do you deliver on time? Have you had problems with delivering products?

What makes a great pitch?

Provide a point of difference, know your product and already know what the best sellers will be. Be confident with the range and build a good rapport with the buyer. It is important to have a good relationship with the customer. If you can see the product in action either on the catwalk, on a model, or actually using it (if it is hardware) then that will build the buyer's association and allegiance with the product.

Another big draw card is to see enthusiasm from the pitcher for the brand and its concepts on a personal level. In the end, the pitcher is often the person that is going to be the contact point between the brand and your organisation. Enthusiasm for the brand often results in enthusiasm and success in the resultant relationship.

Is there a particular past pitch that sticks out in your memory? If yes, why?

Alpinestars invited Surfdome to the Moto GP, where they presented their clothing range and then in turn we saw the product in action. For Surfdome it was a great experience to go to a moto-sport event, but it also built a strong association between the brand and the brand's market in the buyer's mind. We were able to see the demographic at the event who are wearing the product, to meet the ambassadors and to see the elite product in action.

If you could give one piece of advice about pitching a product to a retailer what would it be?

Be confident with your pitch, know your prices both retail and trade, know the retailer you are going into, understand the gaps in the market and in the retailers' store. Where possible have a rainbow range or have the correct prototype of hardware so that the retailer knows that what they are seeing is the product that is going to be delivered.

Part Three

After A
Successful Pitch

Chapter 6

Continue to Push Your Brand and Products

If all has gone to plan you have hopefully now been listed by at least one major retailer. If this is the case, congratulations!

But having achieved this, now is not the time to relax. Now is the time to really start pushing your brand and being as proactive as possible. You have to work hard so that your stockist sells enough units for them to warrant another order. To enable that to happen it is imperative that you start raising your brand awareness in any way possible. You now need to make a wider consumer audience aware of your product, its benefits and where they can purchase it.

You may feel that it is the responsibility of the retailer to sell your product to customers, and to a certain extent it is. They will help to promote your product as it's in their best interest to do so, but the responsibility also falls on you to spread the word.

A potential problem you may face is that your business has started to grow and you are spending more and more time dealing with the everyday care and attention it requires, whilst still aiming to get in front of additional retailers. You may not be quite big enough to start employing a management team just yet and you probably don't really want to relinquish control at this delicate stage, so what other options do you have? Now is the time to consider either employing somebody to take care of your publicity (also known as public relations, or PR) or to outsource it elsewhere.

Outsourcing PR

If money is still tight, outsourcing your PR requirements is the perfect solution. Many PR specialists offer a multitude of packages with price ranges to suit any growing business. You could start with simply having a few press releases written, sent out and followed up, or you could go for a complete remote press office.

The first thing you need to decide is who you would like to have representing your business. A good place to start is by asking some of the contacts you have built up for recommendations. When you have a shortlist of potential PR representatives, there are two main things that you need to confirm:

- Ensure that you find a business to consumer PR expert as opposed to a business-to-business specialist.
- Ensure that they are familiar with and have experience dealing with your industry.

Don't be embarrassed or feel awkward asking PR businesses for references. If they are good at what they do they should have them in abundance.

Business to consumer PR specialist Lesley O'Mara, founder of LS Media (**www.lsmedia.co.uk**), says:

"Once a major retailer has agreed to stock your product, you need to let your customers know it's there. One of the most effective ways of communicating this is through a strategic PR campaign, aimed ultimately at generating print, broadcast and online coverage.

"As well as being effective at delivering factual messaging such as price point, stockist information, etc., PR gives you the opportunity to bring your brand to life by aligning the product with certain news angles, people or third party brands which help enhance its reputation. By influencing the right journalists or bloggers, and generating product reviews or round-ups, your product starts to be seen in the right places by the right people.

"Secondary to letting people know your product exists, PR can also be influential with existing and prospective retailers: press coverage builds product demand; customers will begin to actively seek out the

product in their stores, asking for it by name as a result of seeing it featured in their favourite magazine or having read about it on a popular blog.

Over and above advertising, PR allows you to deliver a much deeper set of messages, bringing the entire brand to life with a personality and tone of voice which can't be achieved through advertising alone. It is also a way of bringing those influential writers on-side: getting their buy-in to your product is often as important as securing that lucrative deal with a high-street retailer."

Marketing activities you can do yourself

Aside from employing a PR expert, there are many marketing activities you can carry out yourself. Some are a little expensive but others can be done with little or no expenditure:

* *Social media plays a huge roll in raising awareness of your brand and your products.* Start Facebook groups dedicated to your product or your brand and get people to join. Run competitions to win a prize to encourage more people to 'like' your page and therefore increase your brand awareness amongst the public. Ask existing friends and family to ask their friends to join your page, and this should start a snowball effect. All of these things take minimal time and effort but all are massively important in ensuring the buying public are aware of your product. All of these principles can be used on sites such as Twitter and LinkedIn too.

* *Offer to do in-store demonstrations or promotions free of charge.* This requires you spending a morning, afternoon or even a whole day in a store promoting your product. Chat to the general public and show them how your product works and explain all of its benefits. This procedure is much the same as pitching your product to a store's buyer. It may be less formal but it is still important to get it right and direct customer feedback is vital. For every purchase made, the chances of you getting a re-order increase.

- *Offer to go in before the store opens or on a training day and talk to the sales staff about your product.* Make them love it as much as you. Ensure that they can see all of the benefits it has to offer as these people will be representing you and your brand out on the shop floor. They will be selling on your behalf and you do not want them to get the details wrong or mis-sell the item.

- *Add details of all stockists to your website.* Ensure that there are addresses and phone numbers for each store that is holding stock as well as links to all websites that have an online shop facility. You may wonder why someone would go to an external site when you are offering the same product on your site. It may be that they have gift vouchers for that particular retailer or they may have a free delivery code for online orders, or they may simply be loyal customers, etc.

- *Exhibit at relevant shows.* There are an enormous amount of exhibitions oriented at the consumer market and each focuses on a specific sector. By exhibiting at a show that is already well established you can demonstrate the best of your product directly to your target consumer. They have probably paid for tickets to attend these shows, which proves that they have an interest in the products being sold in your sector. For instance, if you are exhibiting at a baby show the people attending are probably intending to buy baby products now or at some point in the near future. Speak to as many attendees as possible and ensure you have enough literature to hand out to everyone. Most visitors will forget you by the end of their time at the exhibition and will only remember those who have given them something to take away.

Doing all that you can to market your product not only keeps your brand at the forefront of consumers' minds but also shows retailers that you are working hard to further the success of your business and, in return, their investment.

Be prepared for further orders

Let's assume your product has been a huge hit with retailers and the buying public and you are now in the position where you are no longer chasing orders but they are coming to you with minimal effort on your part. Once more your organisation and communication skills are key in this situation.

When you originally pitched your product to the buyer, you would have given them estimated delivery times on all future orders to be placed, and these predictions will now be tested. Once you have a second order from a retailer you know that they like your product, it's selling, and they have the confidence to start ordering on a regular basis.

Upon receipt of a new order, check any pending orders that you currently have. Once done, check your stock levels against these orders. If you have enough stock left over to complete the new order within a week but the agreement is delivery within four weeks, don't be tempted to start sending completed orders out just yet. Also, check whether there are delivery restrictions, with Amazon and WHSmiths, for instance, you might have a 2 hour delivery slot on a set day. The bigger the chain the more likely this is.

Contact your manufacturer and confirm delivery schedules of products to you. If you have an order being delivered within two weeks just hold fire until you have the new stock and then despatch your order. If you are told that your manufacturer will have stock delivered to you within four weeks, wait a fortnight and then send your existing stock to the retailer knowing that you will be taking delivery of more soon.

You might be asking why these steps are necessary.

Imagine a scenario where your highest ordering retailer calls you stating that they have run out of stock faster than anticipated and need some more immediately. They have a purchase order ready and waiting to be signed off but need to know the fastest delivery you can do. It would be awful to then have to tell them that they must wait the usual four weeks before they will receive anything.

It's much better to be prepared for this than risk upsetting your important partners.

Have a contingency plan in place to ensure that your stockists are looked after and make sure they know that should the day ever arrive where they are in desperate need of additional stock to be delivered within a few days, there is a possibility that you just may be able to fulfil it.

Build a strong relationship with your partners

When you receive a purchase order from a retailer you are at the start of what will hopefully become a very fruitful business relationship and like any relationship it needs to be nurtured.

There are lots of things you can do to try and build a great working relationship with buying departments. Send Christmas cards, send a box of chocolates at Easter, call them every month for a progress report and to enquire if there is anything that you can do to help.

You should be just as enthused about the single store retailer who orders 50 units per year as the multinational who orders 50,000 units. Ensure you approach your buyer once a year and offer to take him or her out for lunch to discuss progress and the future. They may say no, but it's yet another reason for you to get in touch and keep your business fresh in their minds. As a bonus, if they agree, you can let them know about the new products you have planned and even attempt a soft pitch.

Your aim is to create a relationship built on trust so that your buyer realises that not only do you know and care about their market but you are actively working on new products that appeal to it.

Retailer case study

- **Name** – Solvej Biddle
- **Company** – Biddle Innovations Limited
- **Position** – CEO
- **Email** – solvej@biddleinnovations.com

What, in your opinion, is the best way to get the name of the correct buyer for your product?

Ask others already supplying that company or go to the senior management and ask them.

Have you found any particular method that gets the attention of buyers via phone or email?

Tenacity is essential – many emails will be ignored but a decent presentation with images and evidence of demand and innovation helps.

Were you asked any questions that you weren't prepared for?

No not really. Before you approach a buyer and certainly before you visit the buyer, put yourself in their shoes and consider the key questions that you would ask if you were buying the product. Also think about what answers you would want to hear! Plan your business strategy in terms of development, marketing, etc., to fit in with what the buyers want.

Did you do anything to make your pitch stand out?

Firstly you must be super confident about your product – you need to exude enthusiasm about it and gather positive momentum.

Structure is essential: state what your product is, what problem it solves, what the market for it is. Prove why they should buy.

Was there a particular part of the pitching process that you found extremely difficult? If yes, what solution did you find?

Nerves can always get people but remember that buyers do actually want to buy good products – this is how they become successful. Help them to identify that your product will improve their range and help them stand out.

If you could give one piece of advice about pitching a product to a retailer what would it be?

Know the market, be prepared and be confident.

Chapter 7

Developing Your Business Further

Expand the number of resellers

Once you have a major retailer placing orders for your products this can impact hugely on all future pitches and proposals. If a well-known business has ordered your produ cts on more than one occasion this shows that not only was it worth their while taking the risk in stocking your products in the first place, but also that they are also selling well enough for additional orders to be placed. From a buyer's perspective, if they can see that another retailer is successfully stocking your product they can place an order knowing that your product is selling well and that they can take a piece of the market.

Once again, you will need to help with marketing to let people know that new stores are carrying your product. You may be aware of JML (**www.jmldirect.com**), a business that is effectively a distributor of products. They sell a variety of products through retail stores and have consistent television marketing campaigns making consumers aware of where to purchase the products. At the end of each advertisement they give the name of each stockist and show all of the store branding.

You may not be able to afford to start booking television advertising campaigns but you can still use JML as an example. Make sure that you have the branding of each retailer that stocks your products on your website, with links through to their online store. Make sure any literature you have printed contains the details of all stockists and be sure to let your resellers know that you are promoting them as stockists of the product.

When pitching to new retailers make a point of stating the names of all of the major stores already stocking your products – this not only adds weight to your pitch but also demonstrates that you have systems in place to accommodate large orders. It shows that you have experience in dealing with larger organisations. Demonstrating that you are confident and capable in dealing with large companies is a positive selling point.

Developing your business

Once you are known by retailers and your product is selling well you must seize this opportunity and start looking at ways in which you can move your business forward.

Since first developing your product you may have thought of ways that it could be improved, you may have come up with an idea for an additional product you could add to the range, or you may have an idea for a completely different product. Whichever scenario you are faced with, start working on it.

You need to make the most of the fact that you are now trusted by your resellers and that you have managed to build a rapport with them. Getting an appointment to meet with them and demonstrate your new product should be much easier than it was the first time around. You may even find that you don't have to do as much of a pitch as before.

You will still need to go through the same process, though, and have everything in place, such as branding, packaging, market research, etc., but this time you will be able to pitch your product in a whole new way.

You can work off the back of the success of your first product. If retailers are still stocking your initial product and it's selling well this shows that you know what you're doing. If you have managed to meet all orders and deadlines this will prove that you are organised and efficient. The fact that you have now developed an additional product shows that you have the sustainability factor. All of this makes you and your products an attractive proposition to a buyer.

Conclusion

If you take one piece of advice from this book it should be that you need to have total confidence in and knowledge of your product in order to sell it to buyers. When you have this confidence and knowledge, you know your product will sell well – it is your business after all, so you must believe it has potential to make you money.

As well as this, you need to have confidence in yourself. People buy from people they like and retail buyers are no different. Show them that you are organised, efficient, reliable and most importantly honest.

On your journey to market you may suffer rejection, just remember that it's not personal and to keep going. Many people are turned down to begin with but they just keep trying and eventually success is the reward. If they can do it, so can you.

Good luck!

BlackBerry

With a BlackBerry® in hand, you have business at your fingertips.

With BlackBerry there is so much you can do;

Work anywhere

- BlackBerry 'push' technology delivers emails wherever you are
- Keep up to date with email, calendar entries, contacts, tasks and memos

Communicate anytime

- BBM™ (BlackBerry® Messenger) – the cost-effective way to keep your business moving
- 'D' and 'R' appear so you know when your message has been delivered and read

Instant access

- With BlackBerry App World™ you can easily get the right apps to help you get the right information, be more productive, responsive and efficient.

Manage your business

- Keep on top of your businesses cash flow, using one of the financial apps to assist you
- Enjoy peace of mind knowing BlackBerry® smartphones have the highest levels of security

BlackBerry® smartphones and solutions are 'built for business', but you can also have fun with a BlackBerry® smartphone. Access the best social networking sites, thousands of apps and great multimedia functions. Check out more on BlackBerry.com and join My BlackBerry to get all the latest news and offers.

www.BlackBerry.co.uk
www.BlackBerry.co.uk/sme
www.twitter.com/BlackBerry

About Brightword Publishing

Brightword publishing is a new venture from Harriman House and Enterprise Nation. Brightword produce print books, kits and digital products aimed at a small business and start up audience, providing high-quality information from high profile experts in an accessible and approachable way.

Our Other Business Bites

Twitter Your Business

By Mark Shaw
eBook ISBN: 978-1-90800-304-1
Print ISBN: 978-1-908003-18-8

Selling for Small Business : A guide to what it takes and how to do it

By Jackie Wade
eBook ISBN: 978-1-90800-308-9
Print ISBN: 978-1-908003-19-5

Finance for Small Business: A straight-talking guide to finance and accounting

By Emily Coltman
eBook ISBN: 978-1-90800-306-5
Print ISBN: 978-1-908003-20-1

Contracts for Small Business

By Charles Boundy
eBook ISBN: 978-1-908003-16-4
Print ISBN: 978-1-908003-21-8

The Small Business Guide to China

By David Howell
eBook ISBN: 978-1-908003-11-9
Print ISBN: 978-1-908003-22-5

Other Products from Brightword

49 Quick Ways to Market your Business for Free: An instant guide to marketing success

By Sarah-Jane White
eBook ISBN: 978-0-85719-144-1

50 Fantastic Franchises!

By Emma Jones and Sarah Clay
eBook ISBN: 978-1-90800-302-7

Go Global: How to Take Your Business to the World

By Emma Jones
Print ISBN: 978-1-90800-300-3
eBook ISBN: 978-1-90800-303-4

Motivating Business Mums: Inspiration, ideas and advice from 45 small business owners

By Debbie O'Connor
eBook ISBN: 978-1-90800-309-6

The Start-Up Kit: Everything you need to know to start a small business

By Emma Jones
ISBN: 978-1-90800-301-0

Little Black Business Books - Networking Step By Step

By Marilyn Messik
eBook ISBN: 978-0-85719-144-0

Little Black Business Books - Setting Up and Growing Your Business

By Marilyn Messik
eBook ISBN: 978-0-85719-157

Lightning Source UK Ltd.
Milton Keynes UK
UKOW030224221112

202567UK00006B/6/P